teacher friend publications

March

a creative idea book
for the
elementary teacher

written and illustrated
by
Karen Sevaly

Copyright © 1988
Teacher's Friend Publications, Inc.
All rights reserved
Printed in the United States of America
Published by Teacher's Friend Publications, Inc.
7407 Orangewood Drive, Riverside, CA 92504

ISBN 0-943263-06-9

TO TEACHERS AND CHILDREN EVERYWHERE

Table of Contents

Making the most of it!

Making the Most of It!

WHAT IS IN
THIS BOOK:

You will find the following in each monthly idea book from Teacher's Friend Publications:

1. A calendar listing every day of the month with a classroom idea.

2. At least four new student awards to be sent home to parents.

3. Three new bookmarks that can be used in your school library or given to students by you as "Super Student Awards."

4. Numerous bulletin board ideas and patterns pertaining to the particular month.

5. Easy to make craft ideas related to the monthly holidays.

6. Dozens of activities emphasizing not only the obvious holidays but also chapters related to such subjects as; Women in History and The Weather.

7. Crossword puzzles, word finds, creative writing pages, booklet covers, games and much more.

8. Scores of classroom management techniques, the newest and the best.

HOW TO USE
THIS BOOK:

Every page of this book may be duplicated for individual classroom use.

Some pages are meant to be used as duplicating masters and used as student work sheets. Other pages may be copied onto construction paper or used as they are.

If you have access to a print shop, you will find that many pages work well when printed on index paper. This type of paper takes crayons and felt markers well and is sturdy enough to last and last. (The bookmarks work particularly well on index paper.)

Lastly, some pages are meant to be enlarged with an overhead or opaque projector. When we say enlarge, we mean it! Think BIG! Three, four or even five feet is great! Try using colored butcher paper or poster board so you don't spend all your time coloring.

Making the Most of It!

ADDING THE
COLOR:

Putting the color to finished items can be a real bother to teachers in a rush. Try these ideas:

1. On small areas, water color markers work great. If your area is rather large switch to crayons or even colored chalk or pastels.

   (Don't worry, lamination or a spray fixative will keep the color on the work and off of you. No laminator or fixative? That's okay, a little hair spray will do the trick.)

2. The quickest method of coloring large items is to simply start with colored paper. (Poster board, butcher paper and large construction paper work well.) Add a few dashes of a contrasting colored marker or crayon and you will have it made.

3. Try cutting character eyes, teeth, etc. from white typing paper and gluing them in place. These features will really stand out and make your bulletin boards come alive.

   For special effects add real buttons or lace. Metallic paper looks great on stars and belt buckles, too.

LAMINATORS:

If you have access to a roll laminator you already know how fortunate you are. They are priceless when it comes to saving time and money. Try these ideas:

1. You can laminate more than just classroom posters and construction paper. Try various kinds of fabric, wall paper and gift wrapping. You'll be surprised at the great combinations you come up with.

   Laminated classified ads can be used to cut headings for current event bulletin boards. Colorful gingham fabric makes terrific cut letters or scalloped edging. You might even try burlap! It looks terrific on a fall bulletin board.

   (You can even make professional looking bookmarks with laminated fabric or burlap. They are great gift ideas.)

2. Felt markers and laminated paper or fabric can work as a team. Just make sure the markers you use are permanent and not water based. Oops, make a mistake! That's okay. Put a little ditto fluid on a tissue, rub across the mark and presto, it's gone! (Dry transfer markers work great on lamination, too.)

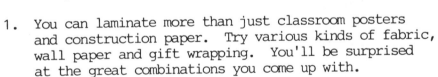

Making the Most of It!

LAMINATORS:
(continued)

3. Laminating cut-out characters can be tricky. If you have enlarged an illustration onto poster board, simply laminate first and then cut it out with an art knife. (Just make sure the laminator is plenty hot.)

One problem may arise when you paste an illustration onto poster board and laminate the finished product. If your paste-up is not 100% complete, your illustration and posterboard may separate after laminating. To avoid this problem, paste your illustration onto poster board that measures slightly larger. This way, the lamination will help hold down your paste-up.

4. When pasting up your illustration always try to use either rubber cement, an artist's spray adhesive or a glue stick. White glue, tape or paste does not laminate well.

5. Have you ever laminated student made place mats, crayon shavings, tissue paper collages, or dried flowers? You'll be amazed at the variety of creative things that can be laminated and used in the classroom, or as take-home gifts.

DITTO MASTERS:

Ditto!

Many of the pages in this book can be made into masters for duplicating. Try some of these ideas for best results:

1. When using new masters, turn down the pressure on the duplicating machine. As the copies become light, increase the pressure. This will get longer wear out of both the master and the machine.

2. If the print from the back side of your original comes through the front when making a master or photocopy, slip a sheet of black construction paper behind the sheet. This will mask the unwanted black lines and create a much better copy.

3. Trying to squeeze one more run out of that worn master can be frustrating. Try lightly spraying the inked side of the master with hair spray. For some reason, this helps the master put out those few extra copies.

4. Several potential masters in this book contain instructions for the teacher. Simply cover the type with correction fluid or a small slip of paper before duplicating.

Making the Most of It!

BULLETIN BOARD
BACKGROUNDS:

Creating clever bulletin boards for your classroom need not take fantastic amounts of time and money. With a little preparation and know-how you can have different boards each month with very little effort. Try some of these ideas:

1. Background paper should be put up only once a year. Choose colors that can go with many themes and holidays. The black butcher paper background you used as a spooky display in October will have a special dramatic effect in December when you use letters cut from holiday foil gift wrap paper.

2. Butcher paper is not the only thing that can be used to cover the back of your board. You might like to try colored burlap. Just fold it up at the end of the year to reuse again.

   Wallpaper is another great background cover. Discontinued rolls can be purchased for next to nothing at discount hardware stores. Most can be wiped clean and will not fade like construction paper. (Do not glue wall paper directly to the board, just staple or pin in place.)

LETTERING AND
HEADINGS:

Not every school has a letter machine that produces perfect 2" or 4" letters from construction paper. (There is such a thing, you know.) The rest of us will just have to use the old stencil and scissor method. But wait, there is an easier way!

1. Don't cut individual letters. They are difficult to pin up straight, anyway. Instead, hand print bulletin board titles and headings onto strips of colored paper. When it is time for the board to come down, simply roll it up to use again next year.

   Use your imagination. Try cloud shapes and cartoon bubbles. They will all look great.

LETTERING AND
HEADINGS:
(continued)

CLASSROOM HELPERS

CLASSROOM HELPERS

2. Hand lettering is not that difficult, even if your printing is not up to penmanship standards. Print block letters with a felt marker. Draw big dots at the ends of each letter. This will hide any mistakes and add a charming touch to the overall effect.

If you are still afraid about free handing it, try this nifty idea: Cut a strip of poster board about 28" X 6". Down the center of the strip cut a window with an art knife measuring 20" X 2". There you have it, a perfect stencil for any lettering job. All you do is write your letters with a felt marker within the window slot. Don't worry about uniformity, just fill up the entire window heighth with your letters. Move your poster board strip along as you go. The letters will always remain straight and even because the poster board window is straight.

3. If you must cut individual letters, use this idea:

Cut numerous sheets of construction paper into 4½" X 6" squares. (Laminate first if you can.) Cut letters as shown in the illustration. No need to measure, irregular letters will look creative not messy.

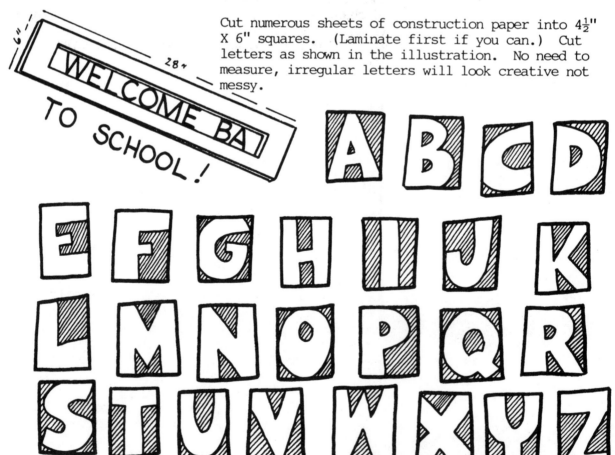

Making the Most of It!

ON-GOING
BULLETIN BOARDS

Creating the on-going bulletin board can be easy. Give one of these ideas a try.

1. Choose one board to be a calendar display. Students can change this monthly. They can do the switching of dates, month titles and holiday symbols. Start the year with a great calendar board and with a few minor changes each month it will add a sparkle to the classroom.

2. A classroom tree bulletin board is another one that requires very little attention after September. Cut a large bare tree from brown butcher paper and display it in the center of the board. (Wood-grained adhesive paper makes a great tree, also.) Children can add fall leaves, flowers, apples, Christmas ornaments, birds, valentines, etc., to change the appearance each month.

3. Birthday bulletin boards, classroom helpers, school announcement displays and reading group illustrations can all be created once before school starts and changed monthly with very little effort. With all these on-going ideas, you'll discover that all that bulletin board space seems smaller than you thought.

Notes

Calendar

- MARCH CALENDAR AND ACTIVITIES

- CALENDAR TOPPER

- BLANK CALENDAR

March

March

1   The first NATIONAL PARK, in the United States, was established on this day in 1872. (Ask students to find out which park was selected.)

2   Today marks the birthdate of THEODORE GEISEL, or as we know him, DR. SEUSS. (Ask your students to list as many of his books as they can.)

3   Today is DOLL'S FESTIVAL DAY in Japan. (Ask all of your students to bring favorite dolls or stuffed toys from home to share with other members of the class.)

4   On this day in 1789, the United States Constitution was put into effect. (Have students find out who was president on this date.)

5   THE BOSTON MASSACRE, an attack by British troops on American colonists, took place on this day in 1770. Crispus Attucks, a black adventurer, was the first to be killed. (Students might like to find out more about Attucks.)

6   "REMEMBER THE ALAMO!" The Texas fort in San Antonio, Texas, fell on this day in 1836 to General Santa Anna and his Mexican troops. (Ask students to find San Antonio on the classroom map.)

7   LUTHER BURBANK, American horticulturist, was born on this day in 1849. (Ask students to find out what a horticulturist does and in particular, what Burbank discovered.)

8   Today is INTERNATIONAL WOMEN'S DAY! (Ask each student to research a famous woman that they admire.)

9   AMERIGO VESPUCCI, Italian navigator and explorer, was born on this day in 1454. (Encourage your students to find out what was named after this famous adventurer.)

10   HARRIET TUBMAN, an escaped slave that helped more than 300 blacks to freedom, died on this day in 1913. (Ask your students to find out more about this great lady.)

11   JOHN CHAPMAN, better known as JOHNNY APPLESEED, died on this day in 1847. (If you didn't celebrate his birthday in September, celebrate today by eating an apple.)

12   The GIRL SCOUTS was founded on this day in 1912. (Ask students to find out more about Juliet Lowe, the organization's founder.)

13   The planet, URANUS, was discovered on this day in 1781 by the German-English astronomer SIR WILLIAM HERSCHEL. (Ask students to locate Uranus on a map of our solar system.)

14   ALBERT EINSTEIN, Nobel Prize winner and father of atomic energy, was born on this day in 1879. (Have students find the meaning to the equation $e=mc^2$.)

15   Today is known as the IDES OF MARCH, commemorating the assassination of Roman emperor, Julius Caesar in 44 B.C. (Have students locate Rome, Italy, on the classroom map.)

16   JAMES MADISON, fourth president of the United States, was born on this day in 1751. (Instruct your students to find out about this president and his accomplishments in office.)

17   Today is SAINT PATRICK'S DAY! (Wear green on this day to honor the Irish gentleman who drove the snakes from Ireland.)

18   The first person to walk in space was Soviet cosmonaut ALEXEI LEONOV, in 1965. (Ask students to find out which American was the first to walk in space.)

19   Today marks the return of the SWALLOWS to Capistrano, California. For more than 200 years, these birds have returned to the same location on this day, each year. (Have students find a picture of a swallow in a book at your school library.)

20   "SPRING" officially begins today in the Northern Hemisphere. (Have students find out which season begins in the Southern Hemisphere.)

21   Today marks the birthday of JOHANN SEBASTIAN BACH, the German composer, in 1685. (In celebration, play one of Bach's many symphonies.)

22   The famous French mime, MARCEL MARCEAU, was born on this day in 1923. (Encourage your students to perform their own mime act for the class.)

23   "GIVE ME LIBERTY OR GIVE ME DEATH," was said on this day in 1771, in a speech to the Continental Congress. (Have students find out who gave this famous speech.)

24   Today is AGRICULTURE DAY in the United States. (Ask students to list all the essential foods that come directly from the American farmer.)

25   Today marks the birthdate of American sculptor GUTZON BORGLUM, in 1871. He was the wonderful craftsman that created the presidential faces on Mt. Rushmore. (Ask students to find out which presidents are represented.)

26   Happy Birthday to Supreme Court Justice SANDRA DAY O'CONNER. She was born on this day in 1930. (Ask students what changes they would like to make if they were to become a Supreme Court Justice.)

27   A major EARTHQUAKE struck the state of Alaska on this day in 1963. (Practice "duck and cover" exercises with your students.)

28   A nuclear power accident happened on this day in 1979 at THREE MILE ISLAND, Pennsylvania. (Ask students to list the advantages and disadvantages of nuclear power.)

29   VIETNAM VETERANS DAY is celebrated on this day by many veterans of the Vietnam War. (Ask students to locate the country of Vietnam on the classroom map.)

30   Dutch artist, VINCENT VAN GOGH, was born on this day in 1853. (Locate several prints of Van Gogh's paintings and display them on the class bulletin board.)

31   The EIFFEL TOWER was officially opened on this day in 1889 during the World's Fair. (Ask students to find out which European city is home to the Eiffel Tower.)

MARCH IS ALSO.....

    NATIONAL NUTRITION MONTH

    YOUTH ART MONTH

    AMERICAN RED CROSS MONTH

    MUSIC IN OUR SCHOOLS MONTH

    RETURN THOSE BORROWED BOOKS WEEK - first week of March

    NATIONAL WILDLIFE WEEK - third week of March

Calendar Topper

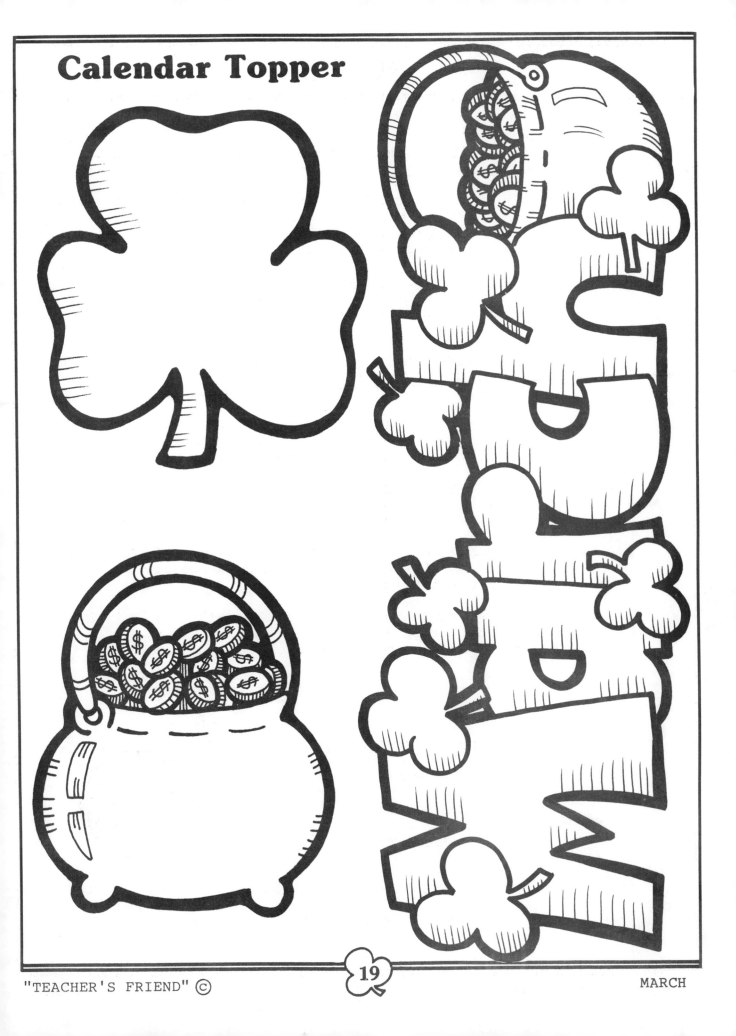

March

sun	mon	tue	wed	thu	fri	sat

MARCH

Spring Activities

- SPRINGTIME BINGO

- AWARDS AND CERTIFICATE

- PUZZLES AND PENCIL TOPPERS

- BOOKMARKS

- MY SPRINGTIME BOOK

- LION AND LAMB

- COLOR PAGE

MARCH

Springtime Activities

During the month of March, spring gently unfolds its colorful beauty. Buds form and open to reveal lovely green trees and multicolored wild-flowers. It's the time of new life! Each new birth of a baby animal or the hatching of a baby bird exclaims that spring has finally arrived.

It's a wonderful time to appreciate nature's beauty and to admire the freshness of everything starting anew. Bring this colorful season into your classroom with these springtime activities and patterns.

Ask your students to do one or more of these springtime activities.

1. Make a list of six ways spring and autumn are different.

2. Ask six people in your class what they like best about spring and write a report about your findings.

3. Write a poem about how you feel about spring.

4. Look up the word "spring" in the dictionary. List the many definitions.

5. Write a story entitled, "The Year Spring Forgot to Come."

6. Find the times of sunset and sunrise for March 21 in the local newspaper. How do these times differ to a month or two ago.

SPRINGTIME BINGO

Your students will enjoy learning more about spring with this spring-time bingo game. Give each child a copy of the bingo words listed below or write the words on the chalkboard. Ask students to write any 24 words on his or her bingo card. Use the same directions you might use for regular bingo.

SPRINGTIME BINGO WORDS

MARCH	PLANTS	BEES	ANIMALS
BEAUTY	DAISIES	BUTTERFLIES	BABIES
FLOWERS	ROSES	BUGS	BIRTH
BLOSSOM	POPPIES	WEATHER	LAMB
BLOOM	PANSIES	RAIN	CALF
BUDS	SPROUT	SUNSHINE	COLT
LEAVES	COLOR	UMBRELLA	CHICK
SEEDS	NEW	CLOUDS	BIRDS
FIELDS	FRESH	SHOWERS	HATCH
WILDFLOWERS	INSECTS	DEW	EGGS

This bingo game can also be used to teach vocabulary words or math facts.

MARCH

Springtime BINGO

		FREE		

MARCH

Awards

_____
Date

_____
Name

WAS A RAY OF SUNSHINE
TODAY!

Name

WAS A REAL
"LIFT" IN
CLASS TODAY!

_____

_____

_____
Name

WAS A TERRIFIC
STUDENT TODAY!

_____
Date

_____

_____

YOU DID A
GREAT JOB
TODAY!

_____

_____
Name

MARCH

Springtime Puzzles

Unscramble these springtime words. The first letter has already been decided for you to make your job a little easier.

WEROLFS   F _ _ _ _ _ _

NUSNESHI   S _ _ _ _ _ _ _

RDBIS   B _ _ _ _

VEALSE   L _ _ _ _ _

TTREBUIESFL   B _ _ _ _ _ _ _ _ _ _

EBSE   B _ _ _

GNIPRS   S _ _ _ _ _

ACTIVITY 1

HELP THE BEE
FIND HIS WAY
TO THE FLOWERS!

ACTIVITY 2

ACTIVITY 3

SPRINGTIME HIDDEN MESSAGE

The letters below form a complete sentence. There is one extra letter that appears again and again. Find this extra letter, cross it out and the sentence will be easy to read.

M F A F R C F H C F O M F E S I F N
L F I K F E A F L I F O N F A N F D
G F O E F S O F U T L F I K F E A
F L F A M F B.

Write the sentence on the lines below.

_____

_____

_____

MARCH

Pencil Toppers

Reproduce these "Pencil Toppers" onto construction or index paper. Color and cut out. Use an art knife to cut through the Xs.

Slide a pencil through both Xs, as shown.

Give them as student awards or birthday treats.

Bookmarks

READ A
BOOK
AND
SHINE!

READ
ABOUT

ST.
PATRICK'S
DAY

IN
THE
LIBRARY !

Name

Name

**FLY
HIGH!**
with books
from the library!

MARCH

Matching Umbrellas

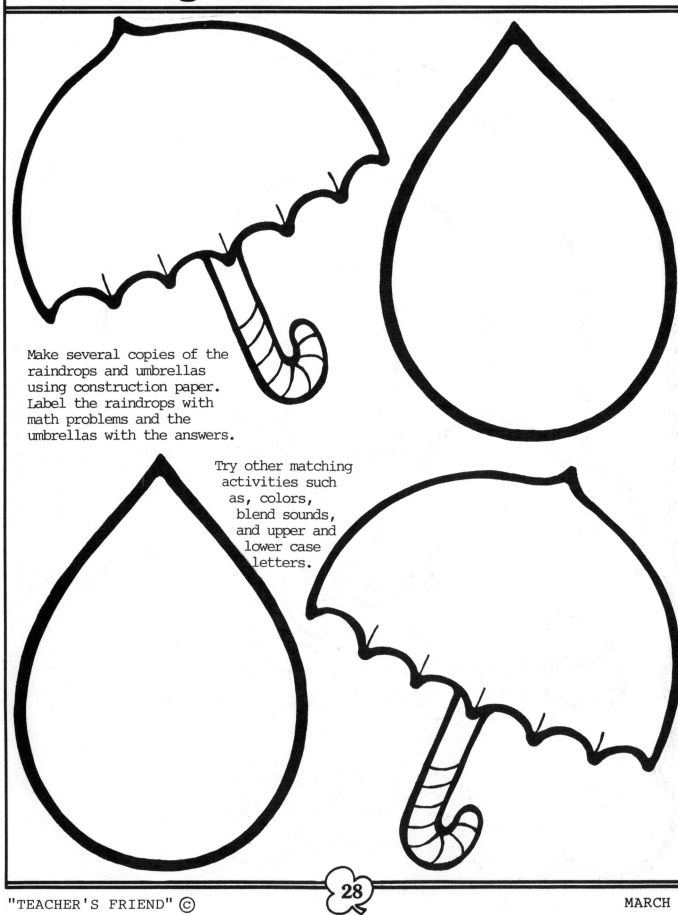

Make several copies of the raindrops and umbrellas using construction paper. Label the raindrops with math problems and the umbrellas with the answers.

Try other matching activities such as, colors, blend sounds, and upper and lower case letters.

Name

My Springtime Book

MARCH

Lion

Lamb

CERTIFICATE OF Achievement

is presented to

_____

For being a Successful Member of the Team!

_____
TEACHER

_____
PRINCIPAL

MARCH

March comes in like a lion and goes out like a lamb.

Write your own springtime similes.

_____

_____

_____

_____

_____

_____

_____

_____

_____

_____

_____

_____

_____

_____

_____

_____

_____

_____

_____

_____

_____

_____

MARCH

Springtime Color Page

Teachers: Add your own math problems to this Springtime Color Page. Children can color in the picture when work is completed.

St. Patrick's Day

- IRISH FUN

- SHAMROCK PATTERN

- MY LEPRECHAUN BOOK

- CREATIVE WRITING SHAMROCKS

- MOVABLE LEPRECHAUN

- LEPRECHAUN WHEEL

- LEPRECHAUN GAMEBOARD

- INTERNATIONAL CHILDREN

MARCH

St. Patrick's Day

Saint Patrick

St. Patrick's Day is celebrated each March 17th in honor of Ireland's patron saint, Saint Patrick.

Patrick was born of wealthy parents, in England, about 385 A.D. His full name was Magonus Sucatus Patricius. When Patrick was sixteen years old, he was kidnapped by Irish pirates and eventually sold as a slave.

For several years, Patrick worked as a shephard in northern Ireland. It was during this time that he decided to devote his life to Christ and teach the Irish his faith. After much hardship, Patrick escaped his captors and fled to France where he began studying for the priesthood. He soon returned to Ireland where he taught the Irish to read and write along with the teachings of Christianity.

It is believed that Saint Patrick was responsible for bringing the small shamrock plant to Ireland. He often used the shamrock in his sermons to illustrate the message of the holy trinity. Today, the shamrock is the national flower of Ireland.

Most historians do not believe the many stories about St. Patrick. But one thing is sure, on March 17th, with many festive gatherings and much merrymaking around the world, everyone is Irish!

Leprechauns

As legend states, every leprechaun has a pot of gold hidden in a secret place, and if captured, he must give up his golden treasure. Of course, it's quite difficult to catch a leprechaun. They are especially tricky and can often turn themselves into rabbits or squirrels to fool you into thinking they are something they aren't. When they are caught, however, they often trick their captor into looking away, for a split second, so that they can make their escape into the woods.

One tale is told of an Irish gentleman, after much searching and effort, captured one of the wee folk. After much coaxing, the Irishman finally persuaded the leprechaun to take him to the very bush where his treasure of gold was buried. It is said, that the man quickly tied a red bandanna to a branch on the bush and hurried home to fetch a shovel. When he returned a short time later to dig up his treasure, a red bandanna had been fastened to every bush in the forest.

Leprechauns love to play tricks on people, causing them to drop or spill things. They often hide keys and other belongings, just to frustrate us. So, next time you lose a possession that you swear should be right where you left it, don't be surprised if it's only some silly leprechaun having fun and playing tricks to pass the time.

Irish Fun

Leprechaun Finger Puppet

Irish Jig

Play a recording of a lively Irish tune and teach your class a traditional Irish jig. Follow these simple instructions:

Place hands on the hips, feet together.

Hop on your right foot while placing your left foot in front, heel down.

Hop again and point your left toe in front of your right foot.

Hop a third time and return the left foot to the front, heel down.

Fourth hop returns you to the starting position.

Repeat the steps, hopping on your left foot.

IRISH SCONES

3 cups sifted flour
$4\frac{1}{2}$ teaspoons baking powder
3/4 teaspoon salt
$\frac{1}{2}$ cup shortening
1 cup buttermilk

Mix all dry ingredients and shortening together until crumbly. Add the milk and continue to mix. Roll the dough onto a floured surface and cut with a round cutter. Bake the scones on a cookie sheet at 425° for 15 minutes. Serve with butter and jam. Makes about 30 small scones.

MATCH THESE IRISH WORDS TO THEIR MEANINGS.

ACTIVITY 4

GAELIC	Lively Irish Dance
BLARNEY STONE	Ireland
IRISH JIG	Irish Language
SHENANIGAN	Walking Stick
GNOME	Mischief or Trickery
SHILLELAGH	Kiss it and receive good luck.
ERIN	Dwarf that guards a precious treasure.

Shamrock

My Leprechaun Book

_____

MARCH

Creative Writing Shamrocks

Students will love creating
their own imaginative stories with
these creative writing shamrocks.

Enlarge this pot and display it on the
class bulletin board.   Place the shamrocks
in the pot and ask your students to choose one
to write about when their work is completed.

Students will also enjoy making up their own story
starters to share with friends.

Creative Writing Shamrocks

... there was a leprechaun that forgot where he hid the pot of gold!

... there was a King that loved the color green!

... there was a troll that stole the blarney stone!

... there was a witch that made a magical soup!

"TEACHER'S FRIEND" ©   MARCH

... there was a fairy that forgot how to fly!

... there was a wizard that cast a spell on the leprechauns!

... there was a leprechaun that lost his magic powers!

... there was a princess that couldn't stop laughing!

Movable Leprechaun

Cut the Leprechaun from index paper and color with markers or crayons. Gold glitter can be used to brighten his buckles.

Assemble with brass fasteners and hang by a string in a window.

MARCH

Leprechaun Wheel

CUT OUT

CUT OUT

Copy this "Leprechaun Wheel" onto heavy index paper. Color, cutout and assemble with brass fasteners. Cut out the two boxes, as shown.

Add your own math problems or word contractions to the wheel. Move the pot of gold to reveal the correct answer.

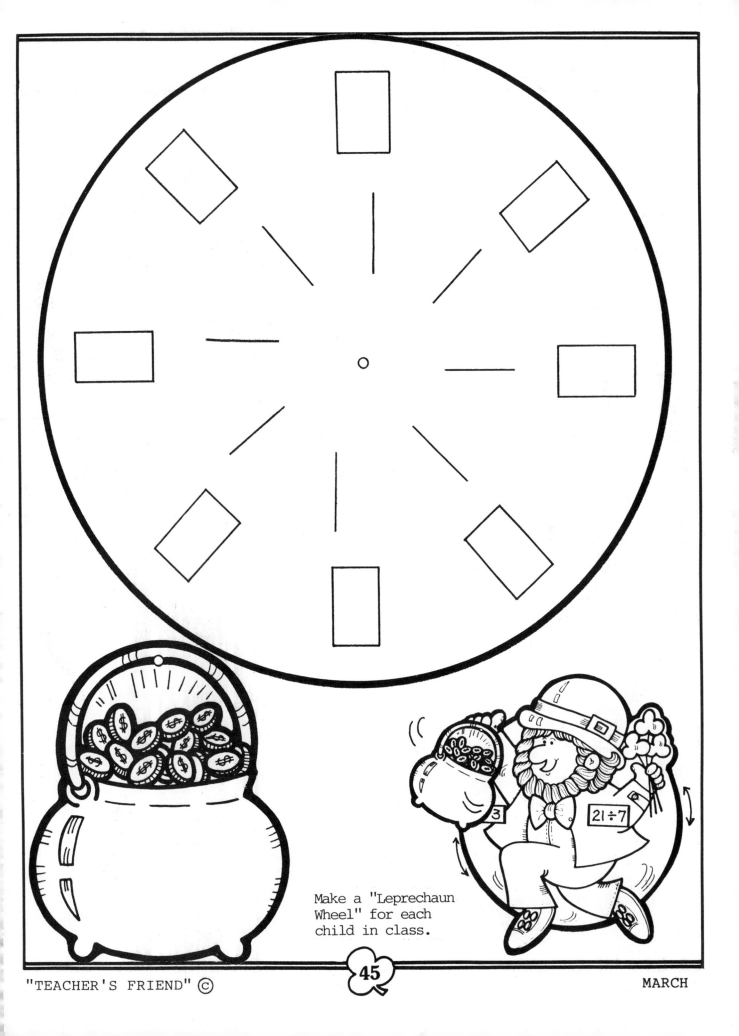

Make a "Leprechaun Wheel" for each child in class.

Help the leprechaun find the pot of gold!

MARCH

"TEACHER'S FRIEND" ©   MARCH

Leprechaun Patterns

Use these cute leprechauns to decorate class calendars or bulletin boards.

Bouquets of paper shamrocks can be placed in their hands.

Leprechaun Stories

Use several of these St. Patrick's Day words in your story: GREEN, LUCKY, CHARM, LEPRECHAUN, SHAMROCK, GOLD, TREASURE, IRELAND, TRICKS, EMERALD, ST. PATRICK.

The Weather

- WEATHER SYMBOLS

- UMBRELLA PUPPET

- CLOUD TYPES

- WATER CYCLE

- THERMOMETER

- PINWHEEL

- WEATHER CERTIFICATE

- WEATHER MOBILE

- MY WEATHER BOOK

- CREATIVE WRITING RAINDROPS

Weather Symbols

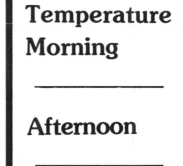

**Temperature
Morning**

_____

Afternoon

_____

**Wind Direction
North
South
East
West**

Use these weather symbol cards to create an informative bulletin board
in your classroom. Each morning, ask a child to go outside and report
to the class the type of weather he finds. Have him or her choose the
appropriate weather symbol and attach it to the class calendar. The
student should also record the temperature and the wind direction. Later
in the afternoon, ask another child to follow the same procedure. Discuss these weather changes with your class. Older children might like
to bring in the weather section of the local newspaper and compare their
predictions and the accuracy of the weatherman to the actual conditions.

MARCH

Umbrella Puppet

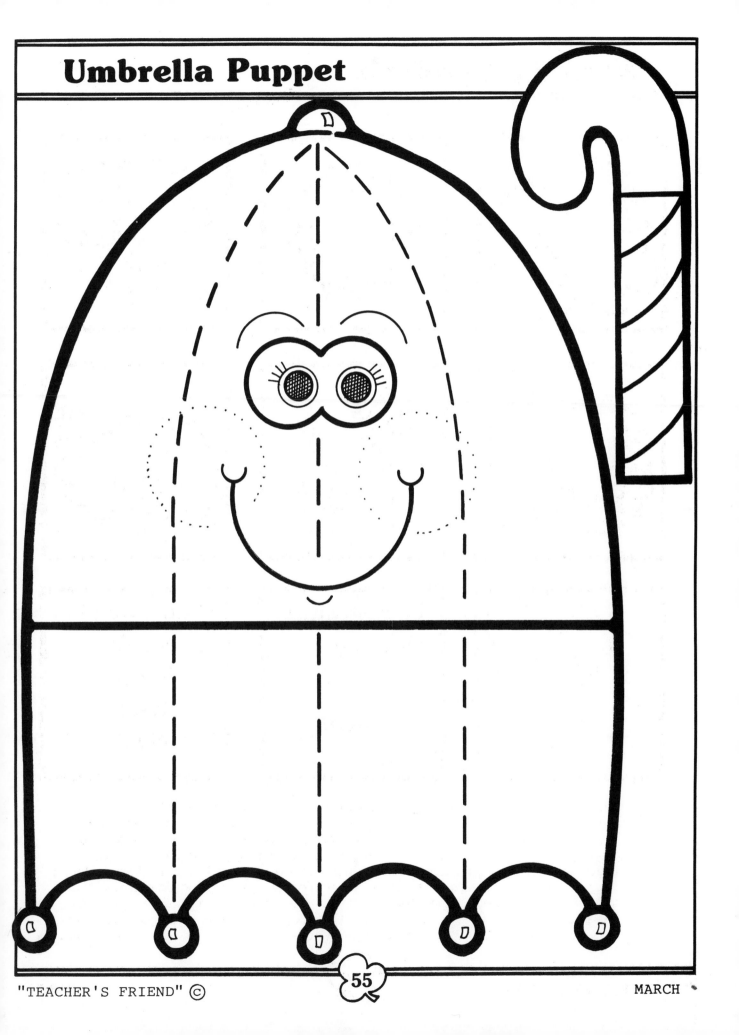

MARCH

Cloud Types

Help students identify different cloud types by having them match the cloud description with the appropriate cloud illustration and name.

These clouds most often appear in the spring or summer on sunny, bright days.

They look like white, puffy heaps of cotton that often resemble animals and other shapes. Many of these clouds tower to 12,000 feet in the air.

These clouds usually appear on fair days against a bright blue sky.

These small, fluffy white clouds often form rows that sometimes resemble the scales of a fish. This is where the term "mackerel sky" originated.

This cloud is most often seen in the summer at the end of a hot day. It is usually called a "Thunderhead" and is the sign of the approach of an electrical storm with thunder and lightning.

This cloud is often in the form of an anvil with heaps of clouds turning first to light gray and then darker and darker.

These thin, white wispy clouds usually appear against a bright blue sky, but may be a sign of approaching rain or snow.

These clouds are found high in the atmosphere at heights of more than 24,000 feet. They also travel very fast and reach speeds of more than 200 miles an hour.

These clouds cover a large area of the sky and most certainly mean that rain or snow are on the way.

These long flat clouds have ragged edges and range from light gray to dark gray.

These heavy, dark gray clouds cover nearly the entire sky. They can occur anytime during the year and most certainly mean rain or snow.

These thin layers of gray clouds cover the entire sky. When they are found close to the ground, they are called "fog." A mist or drizzle of light rain is always associated with these clouds.

These cloud cards can also be enlarged and used as an effective class bulletin board display. Use cotton batting for the clouds to create a three dimensional effect. Storm clouds can be tinted blue or gray with dry tempera paint or colored chalk.

CUMULUS

CIRRO-CUMULUS

CUMULO-NIMBUS

CIRRUS

NIMBUS

NIMBO-STRATUS

STRATUS

MARCH

Water Cycle

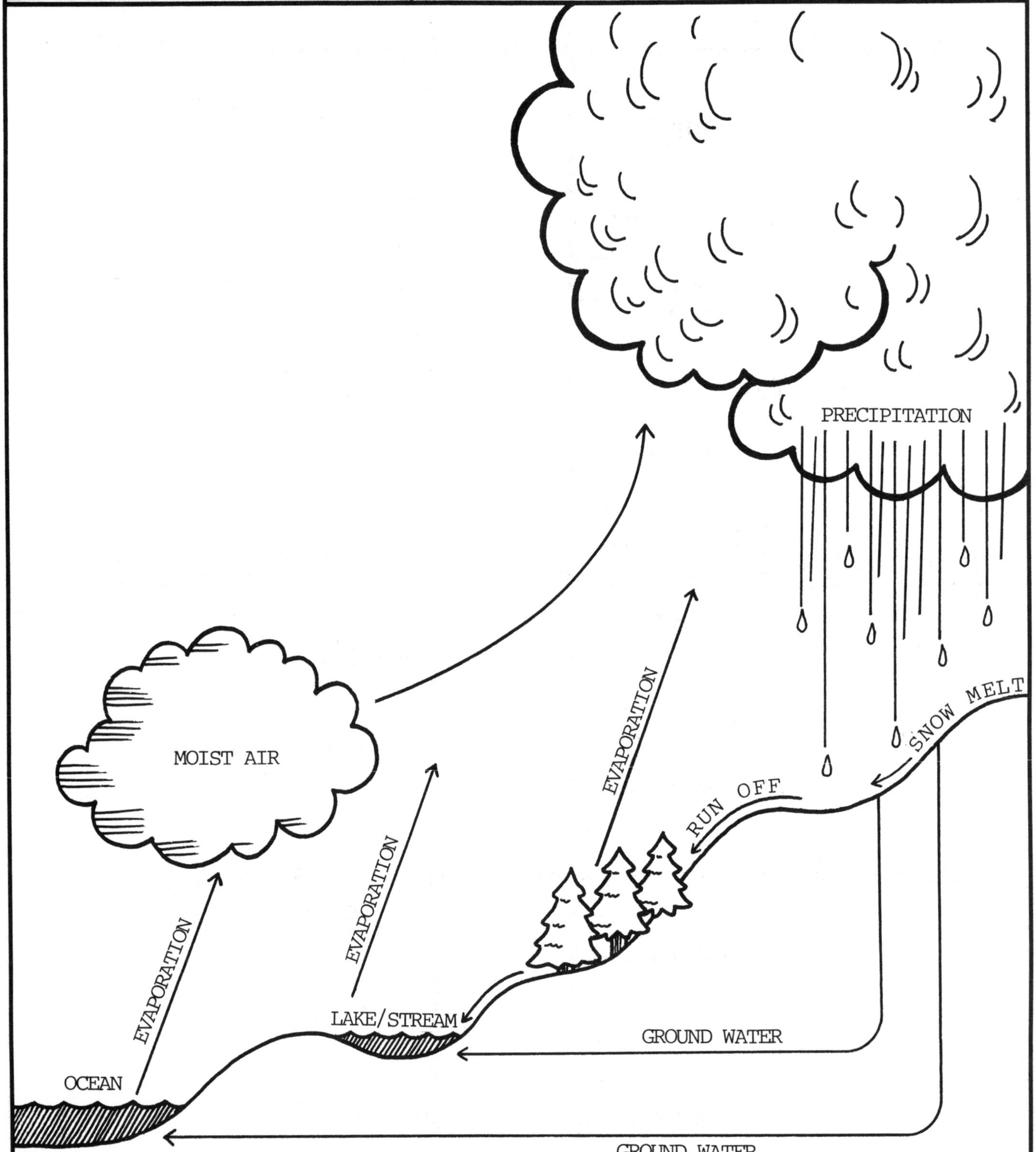

PRECIPITATION

MOIST AIR

SNOW MELT

EVAPORATION

RUN OFF

EVAPORATION

EVAPORATION

LAKE/STREAM

GROUND WATER

OCEAN

GROUND WATER

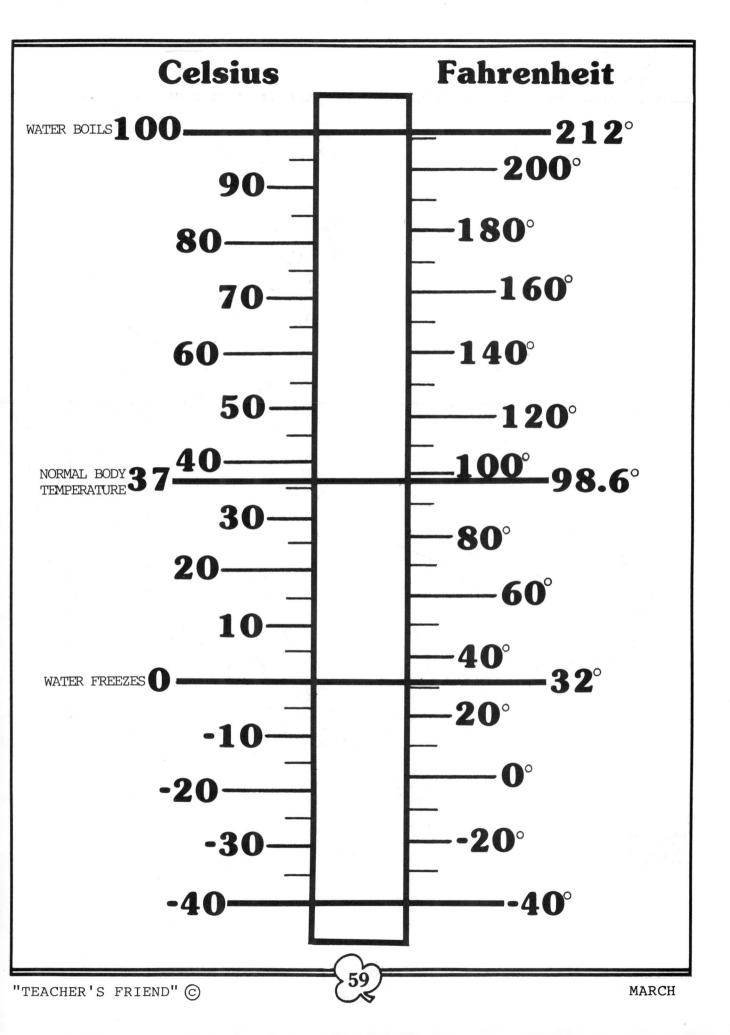

Celsius   Fahrenheit

WATER BOILS **100** ———————————————— **212°**

90 —   **200°**

80 —   **180°**

70 —   **160°**

60 —   **140°**

50 —   **120°**

NORMAL BODY **37 40** —   **100° 98.6°**
TEMPERATURE

30 —   **80°**

20 —   **60°**

10 —   **40°**

WATER FREEZES **0** ———————————————— **32°**

                              20°

-10 —   **0°**

-20 —   **-20°**

-30 —

-40 —   **-40°**

MARCH

Pinwheel

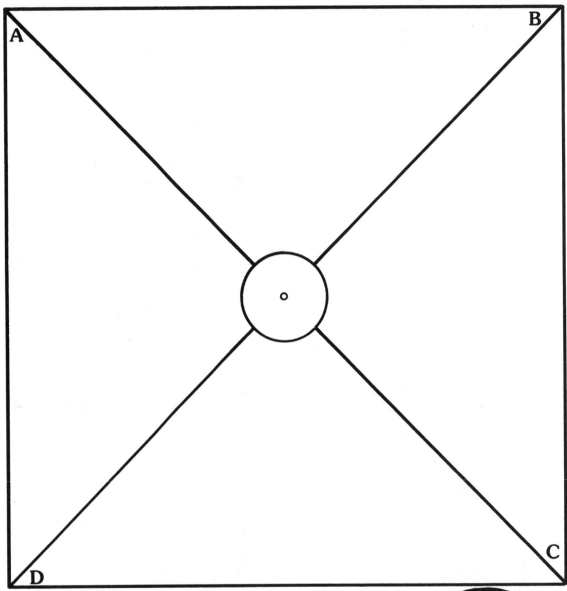

Cut this pinwheel pattern from construction paper and decorate both sides using crayons or colored markers.

Cut along each corner line toward the center, stopping at the larger circle. Bend each corner, (A, B, C, and D) to the center and secure with a straight pin. (Do not fold flat.)

Push the pin into an eraser at the end of a pencil and your pinwheel is ready to spin in the wind!

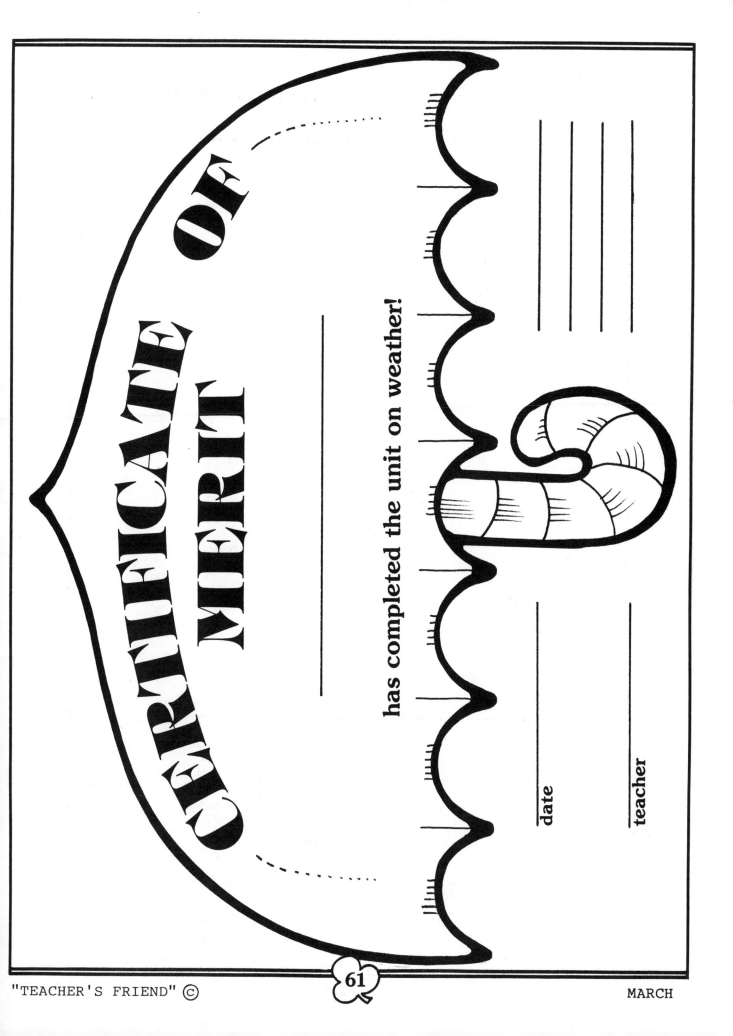

CERTIFICATE
OF
MERIT

has completed the unit on weather!

date

teacher

MARCH

Weather Mobile

Each student can make his own "Weather Mobile" using these simple patterns. Cut the patterns from construction paper and assemble with thread or yarn, as shown. (For best results, paste the rainbow pattern to posterboard.)

Discuss with your class the different types of weather. Students might like to write "rainy day" or "sunshine" poems on the back of the mobile characters.

Christmas tinsel, taped to the back of a cloud, is a clever way to represent rain and silver foil, glued to the lightning bolt, creates a dramatic effect. Students will love to experiment with a wide variety of new materials.

Children will love to take this "Weather Mobile" home to share with family members.

This rainbow pattern can also be used to make other springtime mobiles.

Hang stars and shamrocks from the rainbow for a St. Patrick's Day craft or paper flowers for a "May Day" mobile.

"TEACHER'S FRIEND" ©

MARCH

My Weather Book

Name _____

This is what I learned about the weather!

The End

Day One

Today's date _____

☐ sunny ☐ windy

☐ cloudy ☐ snowy

☐ rainy ☐ foggy

☐ other

_____

Highest temperature _____

Lowest temperature _____

Air quality _____

Day Two

Today's date _____

☐ sunny ☐ windy

☐ cloudy ☐ snowy

☐ rainy ☐ foggy

☐ other

_____

Highest temperature _____

Lowest temperature _____

Air quality _____

MARCH

Day Four

Today's date _____

☐ sunny   ☐ windy

☐ cloudy   ☐ snowy

☐ rainy   ☐ foggy

☐ other _____

Highest temperature _____

Lowest temperature _____

Air quality _____

Day Three

Today's date _____

☐ sunny   ☐ windy

☐ cloudy   ☐ snowy

☐ rainy   ☐ foggy

☐ other _____

Highest temperature _____

Lowest temperature _____

Air quality _____

MARCH

Day Six

Today's date _____

- ☐ sunny   ☐ windy
- ☐ cloudy   ☐ snowy
- ☐ rainy   ☐ foggy
- ☐ other _____

Highest temperature _____

Lowest temperature _____

Air quality _____

Day Five

Today's date _____

- ☐ sunny   ☐ windy
- ☐ cloudy   ☐ snowy
- ☐ rainy   ☐ foggy
- ☐ other _____

Highest temperature _____

Lowest temperature _____

Air quality _____

Creative Writing Raindrops

Children will love creating their own imaginative stories using these creative writing raindrops.

Enlarge the umbrella and display it on the class bulletin board. Pin the raindrops around the umbrella.

When work is completed, ask each child to choose a raindrop and write a story about it.

Children might like to write their own story starter raindrops to be used by other students.

The little raindrop couldn't bring himself to fall to earth.

Suddenly, lightning hit the old tree in the front yard!

The
rain came
down like
cats and
dogs.

The
wind blew
my hat
high in the
sky!

The
dog ran in
the house
at the sound
of the
thunder.

The
thermometer
reached
120°!

The Day It Rained....

marshmallows!
lemonade!
jellybeans!

peanut butter!
tennis shoes!
pennies!

Women in History

- WOMAN WORD FIND

- FAMOUS WOMAN CONCENTRATION

- FAMOUS WOMEN PORTRAITS

- MY FAVORITE WOMAN

Women to admire!

- Rosa Parks
- Elizabeth Blackwell
- Shirley Chisholm
- Peggy Fleming
- Sally Ride · Pearl Buck

MARCH

Famous Woman Word Find

FIND THE LAST NAMES OF THESE FAMOUS WOMEN IN THE PUZZLE BELOW:

Mary McLeod BETHUNE
Abigail ADAMS
Coretta KING
Susan B. ANTHONY
Laura Ingalls WILDER
Sandra Day O'CONNER
Sally RIDE
Shirley CHISHOLM

Betsy ROSS
Clara BARTON
Amelia EARHART
Elizabeth BLACKWELL
SACAGAWEA
"Babe" DIDRIKSON
Helen KELLER
Eleanor ROOSEVELT

Harriet TUBMAN
Rosa PARKS
Katherine HEPBURN
Shirley Temple BLACK
Ramona BANUELOS
Wilma RUDOLPH
Pearl BUCK
Sojourner TRUTH

ACTIVITY 5

```
C V G T Y H J N T D C V B L A C K W E L L
H I D R D F G T Y H J U I K L O P M N H Y
I X C U D V K E L L E R S X A W V D R T H
S D E T I S F B U C K F T H Y U K I L O P
H S W H D S V B T S I S W E T U B M A N U
O S W E R D F G T Y N H E P B U R N D W Q
L W S R I S W V B N G H Y F R T Y H N M R
M C B N K D R F V R O O S E V E L T S C I
B A R X S B A R T O N D C C V T Y H U J D
S D O D O X V F G B A N U E L O S S W G E
C T S F N H W I L D E R S P A E W R T H Y
X Z S D F G B E T H U N E A B L A C K P R
R U D O L P H C F G S E T R V B N M K A I
A E A R H A R T S C F T Y K C V B N M R L
Z C D B G H S A C A G A W E A D C V B K Y
S D A V G T Y H J U I K L O P M B G Y S R
B V M A N T H O N Y V T Y U I R E W F D S
M K S F G B H N M J K L I U O C O N N E R
```

SELECT ONE OF THE WOMEN LISTED AND WRITE A BRIEF DESCRIPTION ABOUT HER ACCOMPLISHMENTS.

_____

_____

_____

_____

_____

Famous Women Concentration

Students will love to learn more about Famous Women in History with this "Concentration" activity. At the same time, students will be developing valuable memory skills.

Mount the card sets on poster board and laminate for greater wear.

Two students can play the game by shuffling the cards and laying them face down on a table top. Each player takes turns revealing two cards at a time, trying to match the famous woman card with her achievement card. If the cards match, the player keeps them and selects again until the cards do not match. Cards that do not match are returned to their exact spot and the player forfeits his or her turn to the other player.

The game continues until all cards are matched. The player with the most cards, wins the game .

Additional cards can easily be made by assigning a famous woman to each student in class.

Ask each child to write the name of their famous woman on a pre-cut square of poster board and their accomplishments on another.

Play the same game as described above.

WILMA RUDOLPH	HELEN KELLER	SANDRA DAY O'CONNER
SOJOURNER TRUTH	BABE DIDRIKSON	SACAGAWEA
SUSAN B. ANTHONY	ELIZABETH CADY STANTON	CLARA BARTON
HARRIET TUBMAN	ELEANOR ROOSEVELT	AMELIA EARHART

This talented Olympic athlete was one of 19 children. She overcame childhood paralysis to win three gold medals during the 1960 Olympic Games.

This woman was born both deaf and blind. She overcame her handicaps and taught herself to speak. She gave numerous lectures across the country dedicated to changing society's attitude of the disabled.

This woman was named the first female Supreme Court Justice of the United States.

This woman was born into slavery but later spoke out for human rights. She traveled the country speaking at anti-slavery meetings and helped ex-slaves rebuild their lives as free people.

This woman was the first female Olympic champion. She won gold medals in the 80m, hurdles and javelin, and a silver medal in the high jump, during the 1932 Games.

Without this Indian woman, explorers Lewis and Clark might have never completed their journey of the North-west. She served them as both guide and interpreter during their 8,000 mile expedition.

This woman was a hardy crusader for women's right to vote. She was once arrested for attempting to vote. Her face appears on the dollar coin.

This woman organized the first Women's Rights Convention. She encouraged other women to fight for the right to own property, obtain an education and to vote and hold office.

This courageous woman tended wounded soldiers during the Civil War. She later organized the American Red Cross which provides relief during both wartime and peacetime emergencies.

Before the outbreak of the Civil War, this escaped slave made a total of nineteen trips to the South to lead other slaves to freedom. She was later known as the "Moses" of her people.

This president's wife devoted herself to a career of social reform. After her husband's death, she was appointed the U.S. representative to the United Nations and later became chairman of the Human Rights Commission.

This woman's love for flying led her to many "firsts." She was both the first woman to earn a pilot's license and the first woman to fly solo across the Atlantic Ocean.

MARCH

**WILMA
RUDOLPH**

AMELIA EARHART

SACAGAWEA

HELEN
KELLER

SUSAN B. ANTHONY

Famous Woman

Name _____

Birthdate _____

Education _____

Occupation _____

Portrait

Achievements _____

_____

_____

_____

_____

_____

_____

My Opinion _____

_____

_____

_____

_____

My Favorite Woman

Draw a picture of your favorite woman. Display her picture on the class bulletin board

Name

MARCH

Japan

- JAPANESE POETRY

- JAPANESE CRAFTS

- FISH PUPPET

- ORIGAMI BIRD

- TORII GATE

- INTERNATIONAL CHILDREN

- JAPANESE STORY CHARACTERS

- MAP OF JAPAN

- CREATIVE WRITING LANTERN

MARCH

Japanese Poetry

Japan has given the world many beautiful things. Their culture, traditions and influence have touched nearly every aspect of our lives. The most admired, however, must be in their art, whether it be paintings, architecture, theater, gardens or poetry.

For hundreds of years, Japanese poets have written a special form of poetry called "Haiku." A haiku is a short verse about nature. There is always a special pattern to the number of syllables used in haiku. The first line always contains five syllables, the second line has seven and the third line has five. Ask your students to count the number of syllables in this haiku poem.

> The soft warm sunshine
> gently opens pink petals
> with the hope of peace.

Instruct your students to write their own haiku poems using one of these topics.

raindrops	pond of water	trees	birds
wind	butterflies	flowers	lightning
the ocean	springtime	honeybees	grass
a garden	fireflies	rabbits	mountains

Have your students make haiku booklets for their poems. Ask them to illustrate their poems on the folded pages.

You will need:

    Two pieces of cardboard (3" X 4")
    20" of adding machine tape
    Enough gift wrap or wallpaper to
      cover both sides of the cardboard.
    A piece of ribbon (20" long)

Cover the two cardboard pieces with gift wrap paper and glue the ribbon to the back of the piece that will become the back cover of the booklet.

Fold the adding machine tape into six equal parts, as shown. Glue the ends to the two pieces of covered cardboard.

When dry, fold the booklet together and tie with a ribbon. Write your own haiku poem inside.

MARCH

Japanese Crafts

ORIENTAL FAN

Make a beautiful oriental fan using a 9" X 12" piece of construction paper. Draw flowers or designs on both sides of the paper. Use chalk, crayons or colored markers, if you wish. Fold the paper every 1/2 inch making fan pleats. Staple the pleats together at one end to form your oriental fan.

ABACUS

For hundreds of years, Asians have used a counting tool, called an abacus, to figure mathematical calculations.

You can make an abacus by using a box lid and thirty-six beads or buttons. Punch three small holes in each end of your box lid. With a needle, pull heavy thread through one hole and secure one bead to the outside of the box. Pull the thread back to the inside of the lid and slip the needle through ten of the beads. Thread the needle through a hole on the opposite side of the lid and secure another bead to the outside. (You may want to run the thread back through all of the beads to add extra strength.) Repeat these steps for each row of beads.

Count the beads, one at a time, or do simple arithmetic problems. It is easy for small children to see how seven taken from ten makes three, with an abacus.

Fish Puppet

To the Japanese people, the koi fish or carp, is the symbol of courage and strength. On May 5th, families fly fish kites from flag poles. Each kite represents one boy in the family. It is hoped that each child will develop the qualities of the much admired koi.

Make this fish paper bag puppet by simply cutting the pattern from construction paper and pasting it to a small lunch sack. Color with crayons or markers.

MARCH

Origami Bird

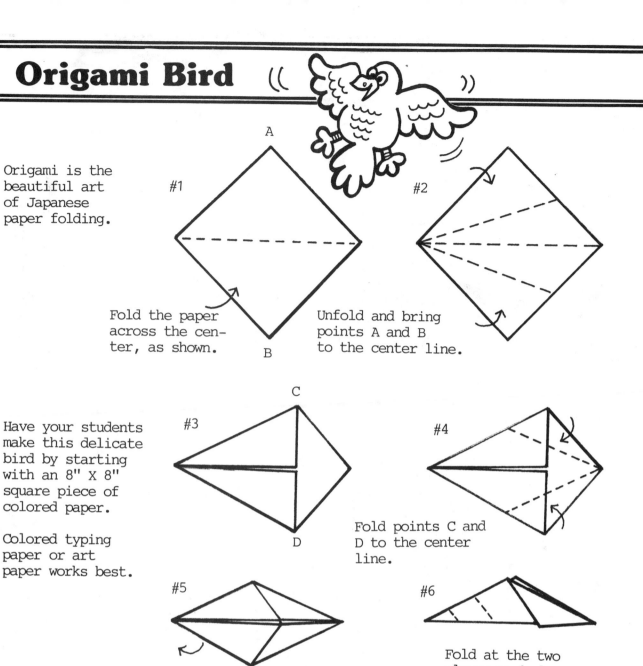

Origami is the beautiful art of Japanese paper folding.

#1

A

B

Fold the paper across the center, as shown.

#2

Unfold and bring points A and B to the center line.

Have your students make this delicate bird by starting with an 8" X 8" square piece of colored paper.

Colored typing paper or art paper works best.

#3

C

D

#4

Fold points C and D to the center line.

#5

#6

Fold at the two places marked on the figure.

It is important that children follow instructions precisely. Do not skip a step, or the figure cannot be completed.

Fold figure in half so that the two flaps resemble wings.

#7

#8

Demonstrate the folding, one step at a time, while your students follow along.

Fold the neck inward and then the head downward, as shown in the illustration.

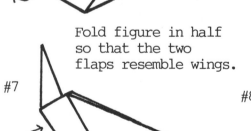

Your finished product is a graceful bird.

MARCH

Torii Gate

Torii Gates are found throughout
Japan. They mark the entry to
Japanese shrines.

It is considered good luck to
walk under a Torii Gate. They
are usually painted red, also
a symbol of good luck.

MARCH

Map of Japan

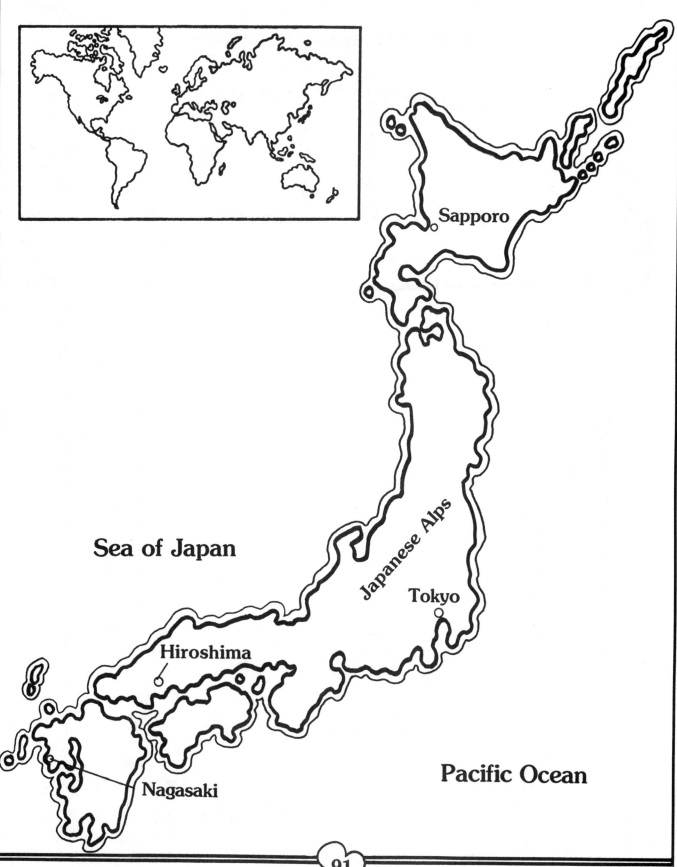

Sapporo

Sea of Japan

Japanese Alps

Tokyo

Hiroshima

Nagasaki

Pacific Ocean

MARCH

MARCH

Japanese Story Characters

MARCH

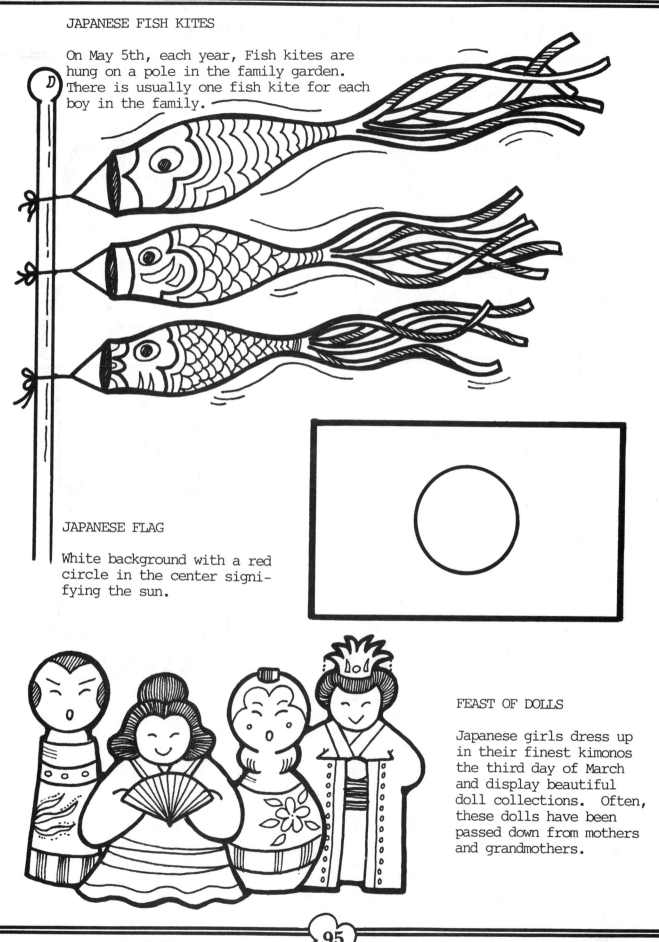

JAPANESE FISH KITES

On May 5th, each year, Fish kites are hung on a pole in the family garden. There is usually one fish kite for each boy in the family.

JAPANESE FLAG

White background with a red circle in the center signifying the sun.

FEAST OF DOLLS

Japanese girls dress up in their finest kimonos the third day of March and display beautiful doll collections. Often, these dolls have been passed down from mothers and grandmothers.

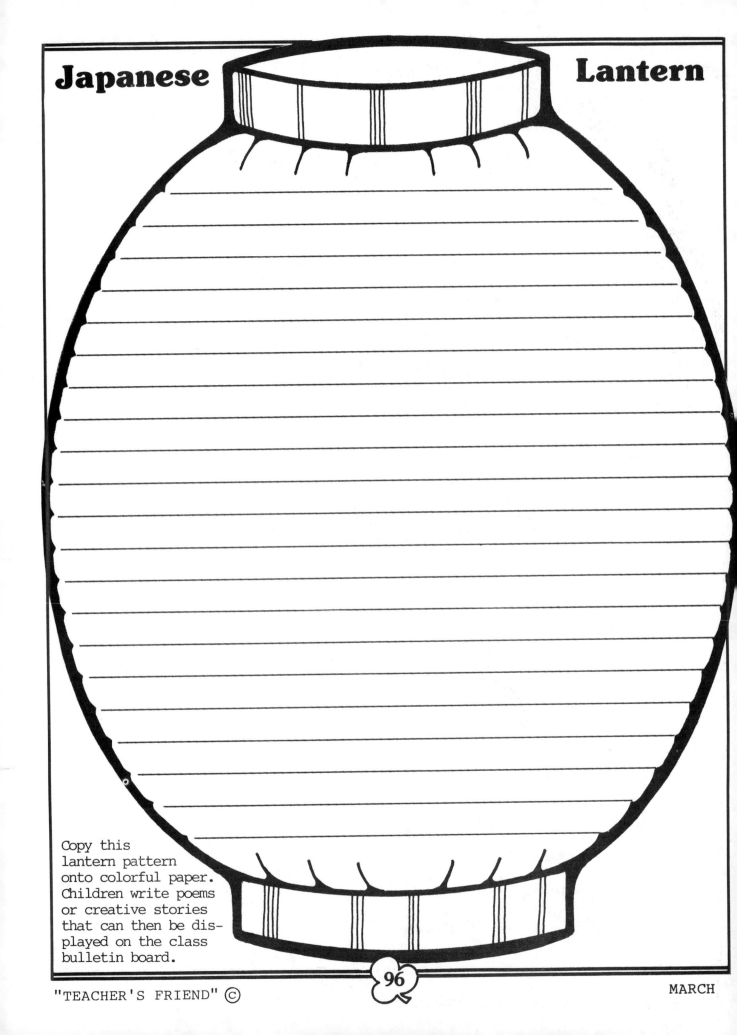

Japanese Lantern

Copy this lantern pattern onto colorful paper. Children write poems or creative stories that can then be displayed on the class bulletin board.

MARCH

Bulletin Boards and more!

Luck of the Irish!

Tony
Jenny
Jimmy
Mike
Kacie
Tiffany
John
Joey
Robbie
Andy

Bulletin Boards

RACE THE RAINBOW...READ!

Display a colorful paper rainbow and fluffy white clouds on the class bulletin board. Student-made raindrops race from one end of the rainbow to the other as library books are read.

DAISY DUTIES

Cut one large construction paper circle and label it, as shown, with the various classroom duties. Cut several smaller circles or petals, one for each member of the class. Arrange the "petals" around the larger circle. Rotate the center circle weekly in order to give everyone in class a turn at the various jobs.

RAINDROP WELCOME

Welcome your students to school this spring with a cute paper umbrella and raindrops. Display each raindrop with the name of a student or ask each child to write a rainy day poem that can then be pinned to the board.

and more...

FAMOUS FEMALES

Ask students to collect pictures and information about famous women. Display these on the class bulletin board along with a large scroll entitled, "FAMOUS FEMALES!"

RAINY DAY MOBILE

Disregard superstition and hang an open umbrella from the class ceiling. Ask each child to write a story or poem on a raindrop pattern and hang them from the umbrella. It's best to use thread or fishing line.

This rainy day display is especially effective when placed over a library table arranged with popular children's books.

SPRING INTO ACTION

Display a cute leaping frog on a class bulletin board entitled "Spring into Action!" Tape small strips of fan-folded construction paper to the back of the frog to give him a "springy", 3-D, effect. Display good work papers around the board.

...and more

The real pot 'o gold!

REAL POT 'O GOLD!

Help children understand the real treasures in life with this simple bulletin board. Display a pot of gold, complete with shamrocks and a large colorful rainbow. Ask students to write values and ideals that are "more precious than gold" on either the rainbow or the shamrocks.

UP, UP AND AWAY!

Large, paper circles are quickly transformed into balloons with this simple idea. Enlarge a cute illustration of a child and display it on the class bulletin board. Place the balloons on the board with long sections of yarn or kite string. Label the balloons with book titles, students' names, colors, etc.

SWING HIGH! THIS SPRING!

Draw a large swing set on the class bulletin board and ask the students to draw pictures of themselves on art paper. Attach a paper swing to the back of each picture and display them on the board. Yarn can be used in place of the swing's ropes.

MARCH

Bulletin Board Murals

Cover a large bulletin board with butcher paper and ask students to draw appropriate murals using colored chalk. Each day, more detail can be added. Students will love adding farm animals, leprechauns or fish kites to the completed projects.

MARCH

Frog Patterns

MARCH

Enlarge this little girl on the class bulletin board and attach colorful balloons to her extended hand.

Door Sign

Let others know when your class is visiting the library or out for P.E.

Mount on posterboard. Cut out the circle and hang on the class door knob.

We'll be back soon. We've gone to...

MARCH

Springtime Babies

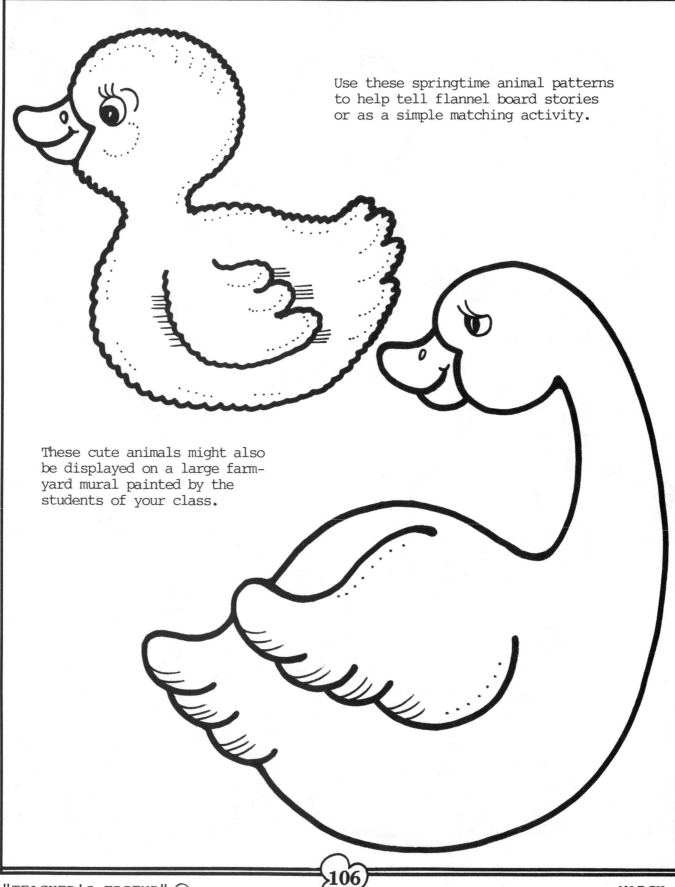

Use these springtime animal patterns to help tell flannel board stories or as a simple matching activity.

These cute animals might also be displayed on a large farm-yard mural painted by the students of your class.

MARCH

MARCH

MARCH

Answer Key

ACTIVITY 1

Unscramble these springtime words. The first letter has already been decided for you to make your job a little easier.

WEROLFS   F L O W E R S
NUSNESHI   S U N S H I N E
RDBIS   B I R D S
VEALSE   L E A V E S
TTREBUIESFL   B U T T E R F L I E S
EBSE   B E E S
GNIPRS   S P R I N G

ACTIVITY 2

HELP THE BEE FIND HIS WAY TO THE FLOWERS!

ACTIVITY 3

SPRINGTIME HIDDEN MESSAGE

The letters below form a complete sentence. There is one extra letter that appears again and again. Find this extra letter, cross it out and the sentence will be easy to read.

MFAFRCFHCFOMFESIFN
LFIKFEAFLIFONFANFD
GFOEFSOFUTLFIKFEA
FLFAMFB.

Write the sentence on the lines below.

March comes in like
a lion and goes
out like a lamb.

MARCH

Answer Key

ACTIVITY 4

MATCH THESE IRISH WORDS TO THEIR MEANINGS.

GAELIC — Irish Language

BLARNEY STONE — Kiss it and receive good luck.

IRISH JIG — Lively Irish Dance

SHENANIGAN — Mischief or Trickery

GNOME — Dwarf that guards a precious **treasure.**

SHILLELAGH — Walking Stick

ERIN — Ireland

ACTIVITY 5

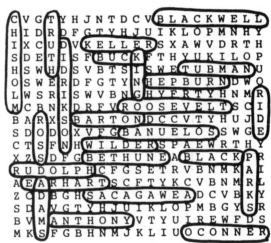

MARCH